Leonardo Boff

Toward an Eco-Spirituality

Translated by Robert H. Hopke

D1523894

A Crossroad Book
The Crossroad Publishing Company

Original publication: *Liberare la terra. Un'ecoteologia per un domani possibile.* Editrice Missionaria Italiana. Bologna, Italy 2014

The Crossroad Publishing Company

www.crossroadpublishing.com

© 2015 The Crossroad Publishing Company

Translated from the Italian by Robert H. Hopke
Study Guide by Robert H. Hopke

Crossroad, Herder & Herder, and the crossed C logo/colophon are registered trademarks of The Crossroad Publishing Company.

Cover design by George Foster

Library of Congress Cataloging-in-Publication Data available from the Library of Congress.

ISBN 9780824520762

Books published by The Crossroad Publishing Company may be purchased at special quantity discount rates for classes and institutional use. For information, please email sales@CrossroadPublishing.com.

He answered them, "When it is evening, you say, 'It will be fair weather; for the sky is red.' And in the morning, 'It will be stormy today, for the sky is red and threatening.' You know how to interpret the appearance of the sky, but you cannot interpret the signs of the times." (Matthew 16:2–3, RSV)

Contents

Introduction

I have worked my whole life on behalf of the poor, who cry out for justice and liberation, along with that of the Earth, which we have been systematically destroying over a number of centuries only to now find ourselves coping with global warming as the result. The theme of my work here is hope: What will the next stage in the life of humanity look like?

There are numerous signs showing us now that an ecological and humanitarian tragedy is on its way. All of humanity is now living in perilous times, with any number of global disasters hanging over the Earth that could well threaten the very existence of our species.

I would like to recall a few essential phrases from the Earth Charter, one of the most profound and beautiful works from this twenty-first century, put forward for the consideration of all civil societies internationally and adopted by UNESCO in 2003. Here we see the values and principles enunciated that will enable us to overcome the current crisis: "We stand at a critical moment in Earth's history, a time when humanity must choose its future. . . . The choice is ours: form a global partnership to care for Earth and one another or risk the destruction of ourselves and the diversity of life." In the face of such dire predictions, I am convinced that hope will win out over fear and that life is stronger than death. Our current suffering is not just a symptom preceding our death but rather an indication of new life, from which I draw the conclusion that the current situation is not an avoidable catastrophe but rather a purifying crisis that might serve as our protection as we move forward to a higher level, rich with promise.

5

So Beautiful Is the Earth

These last centuries of our history have been distinguished by an infinite number of discoveries: continents, indigenous peoples, new species, galaxies, stars, the subatomic world, primal energies and now the Higgs boson, elementary particles that absorb and stabilize matter when contacted. But we did not discover the Earth as a planet, as our shared Home, until we traveled beyond it, and it seems now that it was necessary to leave our Earth and see it from the outside in order to appreciate how we human beings are at one with our planet.

This was the great legacy of the astronauts, who were the first to have the opportunity to contemplate the Earth from outer space, communicating what came to be called "the overview effect." Their beautiful testimony to what they saw was collected by Frank White in his book *The Overview Effect: Space Exploration and Human Evolution* (Bethesda, MD: American Institute of Aeronautics and Astronautics, 3rd ed., 2014), and when we read their descriptions of what they saw, we cannot help but feel powerful emotions and a deep feeling of reverence, hallmarks of a true spiritual experience. Let us consider some of what they have said.

Rusty Schweickart says, "A little later on, your friend . . . goes out to the moon. Now he looks back and he sees the Earth not as something big, where he can see the beautiful details, but as a small thing. . . . The contrast between that bright blue and white Christmas tree ornament and the black sky, that infinite universe, really comes through. . . . The Earth is so small and fragile and such a precious little spot in that universe that you can block it out with your thumb. . . . And you realize from that perspective that you've changed, that there's something new there, that the relationship is no longer what it was" (pp. 36–37).

Eugene Cernan confesses, "When I was the last man to walk on the moon in December 1972, I stood in the blue darkness and looked in awe at the earth from the lunar surface. What I saw was almost too beautiful to grasp. There was too much logic, too much purpose—it was just too beautiful to have happened by accident. It doesn't matter how you choose to worship God. . . . He has to exist to have created what I was privileged to see" (pp. 37–38).

With keen intuition, another astronaut, Joseph P. Allen observes, "With all the arguments, pro and con, for going to the moon, no one suggested that we should do it to look at the Earth. But that may in fact be the most important reason" (p. 115).

Through such a singular experience as they had, human beings come to understand that they and the Earth are one unit; and that this unit belongs to an even greater unity, that of the solar system; and that this unity in turn belongs to another, even greater unity, the galaxy; and that this belongs to the entire universe. which in the end belongs to the Mystery, and the Mystery to the Creator.

"You look back home and you say to yourself," Eugene Cernan continues, "'That's humanity, love, feeling, and thought.' You don't see the barriers of color and religion and politics that divide this world. You wonder, if you could get everyone in the world up there, wouldn't they have a different feeling?" (p. 179).

What they witnessed to from space convinces us that Earth and humanity truly form a single, indivisible whole. That is exactly what Isaac Asimov wrote in the *New York Times* on October 9, 1982, on the twenty-fifth anniversary of the launch of Sputnik, the first human-made satellite to orbit the earth. The title of his article was "Sputnik's Legacy: Globalism," and in it he wrote, "Forced into our unwilling minds has been a view that presents Earth and humanity as a single entity." The Russian Anatoly Berezovoy, who spent 211 days in space, declared the same thing: that it is not possible to separate the Earth on one hand from humanity on the other: together they form one living, organic whole. We human beings are a part of the Earth that feels, thinks, loves, nurtures, and worships.

As we contemplate images of our globe now seen everywhere, they spontaneously evoke in us the awareness that, despite all the destructive threats being launched against Gaia, in some way, a good and beneficent future is guaranteed. Such beauty and splendor cannot be destroyed despite the three structural crises we are now facing: the crisis of sustainable growth, the worldwide social crisis, and the crisis of climate change.

Voices of the Prophets

The prophet, in the biblical sense, is not strictly speaking someone who predicts the future. Rather, he is one who analyzes the present, identifies trends—generally those going in the wrong direction—admonishes, and even at times utters threats. He announces the judgment of God in the course of history and promises liberation from disaster.

From the trends he notes, he envisions the future and fundamentally affirms that "if the leaders of the people continue in this manner of behavior, lethal misfortune will be the result." The transgression of sacred laws lead to disaster, and to make their point, the prophets often paint dramatic scenarios of what is to come in order to call the people back to reason and to an observance of just and right in the sight of God and nature.

In reading some of the prophets of the Old Testament as well as Jesus' warnings concerning future times, it is easy to see our current leaders and their irresponsible behavior with regard to various situations taking shape around the world, in the biosphere, and in the fate of our civilization.

Sometime ago, in various places in the Northern Hemisphere of our planet, we passed a critical limit: that of 400 parts per million of carbon dioxide in the atmosphere. Unfortunately, we are now at that point where only with great difficulty can global warming be reversed. It may be that the situation stabilizes, like that of a chronically ill patient. The temperature of the Earth's surface will rise again another 2 degrees C, and many organisms will be unable to adapt. Because we do not now possess the means to minimize the negative effects, many species will become extinct. The desertification of even greater areas of the earth will continue, harvests will dwindle, and millions of people will need to abandon their homes and countries because of the intolerable heat and the consequent inability to obtain sufficient food.

It is in relationship to a very similar social context that I read the prophet Isaiah, who lived in the eighth century BC—one of the most turbulent periods of human history. At that time, Israel found itself crushed between two world powers, Egypt and Assyria, who were fighting for hegemony over its territory. Each of them invading in turn, they left behind them a swath of destruction and death.

In this dramatic historical context, Isaiah 24 describes a series of environmental disasters. His descriptions call to mind that which might well happen today if the nations of the world do not come together to create an organization that will put a halt to global warming, and in particular those effects as yet unknown, which many notable scientists have predicted and which could become reality before the end of the twenty-first century. Without such action, we risk the decimation of the human race and the destruction of a large part of our biosphere.

The prophets need to be taken seriously. They are discerning trends that go beyond space and time, and thus their warnings are relevant to our contemporary generation. I would like to paraphrase certain verses from Isaiah 24 as both admonition and material for reflection.

"The same will befall the creditor as the debtor. The whole earth will be devastated. The earth has been defiled by its inhabitants, because they have transgressed God's laws, disobeyed His degrees, and broken the eternal covenant. For this reason, the earth will be cursed and its inhabitants will suffer greatly. The earth will fall apart and will be reduced to ashes, it will fall into ruin like a drunk, it will blow in the wind like a curtain. The moon will grow red, and the sun will dim."

Jesus, the last and greatest of the prophets, warns, "For nation will rise against nation, and kingdom against kingdom, and there will be famines and earthquakes in various places" (Matthew 24:7). "Men [will be] fainting with fear and with foreboding of what is coming on the world; for the powers of the heavens will be shaken" (Luke 21:26).

Did we not witness similar scenes with the tsunami in southwestern Asia or after Fukushima in Japan? And what of the great Hurricanes Katrina or Sandy in the United States and those elsewhere on our planet? Were people not overcome with fear at the extent of the death and devastation? These disasters did not happen by mere chance, but they occurred because we have broken the sacred covenant between the Earth and its natural cycles. They should serve as signs and images calling us to responsibility.

Curiously, despite all these scenes of destruction, the prophet's words always end on a note of hope. Isaiah says, "And he will destroy on this mountain the covering that is cast over all peoples, the veil that is spread over all nations. ... The Lord God will wipe away tears from all faces. ... It will be said on that day, 'Lo, this is our God; we have waited for him, that he might save us. This is the LORD; we have waited for him; let us be glad and rejoice in his salvation'" (Isaiah 25:7–9). And Jesus ends by promising, "Now when these things begin to take place, look up and raise your heads, because your redemption is drawing near."

After these prophetic words, any further commentary would be out of place, except that of a mournful and meditative silence. However, let us consider our own era. On September 15, 2008, we witnessed the economic and financial bubble of Wall Street collapse, and a little over one week later, on September 23, we observed what has come to be called Earth Overshoot Day, marking "the day when the natural capacities of the Earth have been exceeded," that moment when the consumption of planetary resources exceeded the natural capacity of the Earth to recover. In 2008, humanity consumed 30 percent more than the Earth could produce. Clearly, the current pace of our exploitation of the Earth is unsustainable. We are consuming reserves of food, water, and raw materials at a rate we cannot continue, for we do not have the means to cover the ecological debt that we are accruing. And yet, as compared to the economic and financial crisis that was on the front page of every newspaper and the leading story of every TV news broadcast, this rather alarming piece of news received scant notice in the international press.

The dwindling resources of our Earth demand that we ask the question: What is more important, to solve the problems that afflict humanity as a whole or to prop up the current economic and financial system? The twenty richest countries of the world (G20) claim, when they meet, that their goal is to rescue this system through controls and corrections, so that it can continue to operate as it did before the crash. The majority of poor and developing countries, on the other hand, are concerned for the future of the biosphere and of life on this planet. If this problem is not solved, the crisis will recur in the form of a collective catastrophe.

In 1961, half of the world's resources were sufficient to meet the needs of humanity. In 1981, all of the world's resources were needed. In 1995, our consumption exceeded production by 10 percent, and even that was sustainable. However, in 2008, consumption exceeded production by 30 percent, and the Earth is giving us unequivocal signals that it can no longer bear up under the weight of such demand. If the rate of gross domestic product continues to grow between 2 and 3 percent per year, as predicted, at this rate in 2050 we will need the resources of two planet Earths to meet the demand for consumption, a scenario that is obviously impossible, if we even survive to that point.

What this all means is that we cannot continue to produce as we have. Our current model of capitalist production is based on the false premise that the Earth is a secure source from which we might draw an infinite amount of resources to produce wealth with the least possible investment in the shortest amount of time. Today, on the other hand, we now realize that the Earth is a small planet, aging and limited, that cannot sustain unlimited exploitation. We need to change our model of production and adopt different patterns of consumption. We need to produce what humanity needs to survive in harmony with the Earth, respecting its limits, in a spirit of equity and solidarity with future generations. This requires a new paradigm of civilization, a globalized model. As Eric Hobsbawm notes in the final pages of his *The Age of Extremes: The Short Twentieth Century*, our world runs the risk of exploding and imploding. It must change. If we do not renounce our negligent ways, the alternative for a change in society will be unrealizable.

Science and Religion Are Allies

I do not wish to linger on the issue of social injustice worldwide, which is a question well known by all. Nearly one half the world lives on the edge of poverty, in hunger and with a chronic lack of drinking water. The data are staggering: 20 percent of the richest peoples consume 84.2 percent of the resources of the Earth, while the poor—20 percent of the world's population—must make do with 1.6 percent of the resources. Such statistics represent a *via crucis* with more stations of suffering and death than the Son of Man Himself walked during his days of passion among us.

These figures are the clearest representation of a criminal lack of solidarity and cooperation on the international level. They reveal us to be cruel and devoid of compassion toward our fellow human beings. Recent statistics from the FAO predict that in the years to come we will need to deal with nearly 150 million to 200 million climatic refugees, individuals who, understandably doing anything they need to do to survive, will cross any and all national borders with the result of destabilizing the political and social systems of many countries. Will we welcome or reject these millions of desperate brothers and sisters?

The worldwide climate crisis has assumed tragic proportions. The Earth is warming. According to the statistics published by the Intergovernmental Panel on Climate Change (IPCC), on February 2, 2007, we passed a point of no return. At this point, our only course of action can be to adapt to the coming changes and seek to reduce their catastrophic effects.

Nicholas Stern, an economist and once vice president of the World Bank and advisor to the then prime minister of England Tony Blair, has calculated the economic effects of global warming, stating that each year we need to invest hundreds of millions of dollars merely to stabilize the rising temperature of the climate to 2 to 3 degrees C, a level that would allow life on this planet to continue. But even if we are successful at this, we nevertheless will still witness the vast destruction of the current biodiversity on earth and the annihilation of millions of human beings whose homelands have become uninhabitable, especially in Africa and Southwest Asia—a virtual holocaust.

Recent data published by the Massachusetts Institute of Technology (MIT) in Boston and by Metoffice in London contain similarly troubling figures. If we do not now take drastic measures to reduce greenhouse gasses, around the year 2035 the temperature of our atmosphere and of the ocean will rise at least 4 degrees C, and by the end of the century, the increase may well reach 7 degrees C, triggering

enormous and catastrophic environmental con-
sequences for life on Earth as we know it. The
scientific community recommends that we reduce the production of greenhouse gasses by 80
percent, but in all the various international meetings that have taken place up to now, no consensus of agreement has been reached, and the
most likely outcome is to agree to a 40 percent
reduction on the part of wealthy nations and 20
percent on the part of developing countries.

For that reason, we deem our leaders irresponsible, especially those of the wealthy nations, who, during their international meetings,
refuse to undertake courageous and effective
action in order to reduce global warming. In
all of human history never have we been faced
with such an important challenge. It is a question of life and death, and it is not possible to
continue to go on living as we have thus far.

In this light, we consider the statements made
by Edward O. Wilson, probably our greatest living biologist. In his book *The Creation: An Ap-
peal to Save Life on Earth*, he states that, for the

first time, human beings have become a geo-
physical force capable of self-destruction. In
order to avoid such a catastrophe, Wilson pro-
poses an alliance between the two major forces
of human culture: science with technology, on
the one hand, and religion, on the other. Religion would help science to act in an ethical
fashion, in the service of life and not in the service of market forces. Science and technology
would help religion go beyond its fundamental-
ist tendencies and to teach humanity to respect
not only the knowledge found in books and in
sacred places but to respect all forms of existence and all that is created. The problem is not
so much how to save the Earth but rather how
to change or our relationship to it. The Earth
itself could continue quite peacefully without
us, while we, however, cannot survive with it.

Liberation theology, the school of thought to
which I belong, was born in the 1960s with the
goal of heeding the cry of the poor, oppressed
women, indigenous peoples, those of African
descent, and other socially marginalized indi-

viduals. Beginning in the 1980s, we realized that the forests, the animals, and indeed the entire Earth itself was also crying, suffering the violence of a destructive industrialized culture. Consequently, in our opposition to poverty on behalf of the poor--the very hallmark of liberation theology—we thus included the Earth among the poorest of the poor, out of which was born a vigorous eco theology of liberation.

Developing Human Capital

Where are we going? No one knows for sure. And yet we can establish at least some preconditions for a new paradigm of livability on our planet.

The socio-ecological crisis that is afflicting every country forces us to rethink our notions of growth and development, as was the case at the UN Conference on Sustainable Development in Rio de Janeiro in 2012, held twenty years after the first such conference in the same city. Our everyday experience brings our awareness to the limits of our Earth. Current models have shown themselves to be unsustainable. Thus, many analysts have stated that industrialized countries must renounce their addiction to "sustainable growth and development" at whatever cost.

In place of the narrow notion of "growth and development," one offers instead the vision of a socio-ecological prosperity that does not entail growth, achieved through an improvement of the quality of life, education, and other non-material benefits. However, poor countries and emerging markets need prosperity with growth. They must satisfy the urgent needs of their impoverished populations. It no longer makes sense to continue to pursue the central goal of consumer-capitalist economic thought, which asks the question, "How can one earn more?" presupposing dominion of nature in service of economic profit. Today, in the face of a changed reality, the question is different: "How do we pursue production while living in harmony with nature, with all forms of life, with human beings, and with the Transcendent?" The answers to these questions will determine whether there will be a prosperity without growth for the developed nations and a prosperity with growth for the poor nations and emerging markets.

To better understand this way of thinking, it is useful to distinguish between four types of capital: natural, material, human, and spiritual. Indeed, it is in the combination of these that prosperity with or without growth is generated. Natural capital consists of all the goods and services that nature freely offers us. Material capital is that which is built by human labor; one needs to consider how it has been acquired and at what cost by way of exploitation or degradation of the natural world. Human capital is made up of culture, the arts, a vision of the world, cooperation—all the realities that belong properly to the essence of what it means to be human.

Here it is important to recognize that material capital has deformed the human, turning the artifacts of culture into merchandise, goods for sale. Yanomami tribal chief and shaman David Kopenawa has written a denunciation of this process in his book *The Fall of Heaven*: "You white people are a people of merchandise, a people who does not heed nature, because you are interested solely in economic advantage" (quote translated from Italian). The same thing must be said of spiritual capital. It, too, belongs rightly to the nature of humanity as a reflection of the meaning of life and of the universe, of what may happen to us after death, and of our highest values, such as love, compassion, and openness to the Transcendent. Because of the predominance of the material, however, the spiritual has been weakened and cannot show us its full capacity for transformation, for creating balance and sustainability in respect to human life, society, or nature.

The challenge today is: How to move from a dependency on material capital to human or spiritual capital? Logically, developing spiritual or human capital does not require making less of the material. A certain level of material development is needed to guarantee a respectable and adequate level of subsistence. Besides, we cannot limit ourselves to growth with prosperity alone, because growth cannot be an end in itself but is part of the overall development of humanity.

In our era, it was Amartya Sen from India, 1998 Nobel laureate in economics, who made a major contribution to an understanding of human development with his notion that development was not merely sustainability but prosperity. The title of his most famous book, *Development as Freedom* (New York: Anchor Books, 1999), is itself the definition of his central thesis. He places freedom at the center of human capital, defining development as "the process of expanding the real freedoms that people enjoy" (p. 3). Likewise, Brasilian Marcos Arruda, economist and teacher, has proposed a plan of transformative education based on praxis and as a democratic exercise of all freedoms.

It is not merely a question of working to increase food availability or toward better health—essential elements of whatever prosperity there is, to be sure. The decisive issue abides in the transformation of the human being. To this end, both Sen and Arruda consider education and participatory democracy fundamental. Education must not be privatized as a product of the economic market (in the form of professionalization) but must be understood as a way of developing and bringing to fruition all the potentialities and capacity of the human being, "whose ontological and historical vocation is to be 'more.' The implication is to better oneself, to go beyond where one is, to activate latent potentialities in one's own being" (M. Arruda, *Educaçao para uma economia do amor. Educaçao da práxis e economia solidária* [São Paulo: Idéias e Letras, 2009], p. 103).

Humanizing the human being is the goal, and in its service are ethical-spiritual values, the sciences, technologies, and our means of production. The political system best suited to foster a sustainable, prosperous human development is, according to Sen and Arruda, a participatory democracy with education. Everyone must feel included in order to build the common good. Human and spiritual capital are such that the more they are used, the more they grow, in contrast to material capital, which decreases as it is used. This may well be the larger message of our current crisis.

3 1

Building a Home for All People

Where does one start, therefore? In the first place, we need a new vision of the Earth, one that understands it as a living super-organism, called Gaia by many biologists and cosmologists, from the Greek goddess of the living Earth. To give a sense of the profusion of life existing here on Earth, according to biologist Edward Wilson, in a single gram of earth there live around 10 billion bacteria of approximately six thousand different species.

Through interdependent physical, chemical, and biological processes, the Earth produces and reproduces life in an ongoing way. Human beings do not merely live on the Earth, but they are the Earth that lives in them, and now, having reached an advanced stage of evolution and complexity, the Earth itself has begun to feel, think, love, and worship. This phase of evolution manifests how human beings rose out of the humus, from the good earth—Adam whose name, according to Judeo-Christian tradition, is derived from *adamah*, fertile earth.

This new vision of Earth actually corresponds to an ancient view of the Earth held by earlier civilizations, according to which the Earth was the "Great Mother" or *Pacha Mama*. Indeed, this view of the Earth as a living being was dominant throughout all of human history up until the arrival of the modern age, when, with Isaac Newton and René Descartes, our earth began to be viewed instead as *res extensa*, a purely physical object devoid of spirit. For Francis Bacon, the founder of the modern scientific method, human beings were called indeed to take ownership of and rule over the Earth, torture and rape it unscrupulously, lay bare all of its secrets. This vision has turned us into the Earth's executioner. Nowadays, we understand that humanity's mission is instead to be the Earth's caretaker and that we are called to live ethically and to be the custodians of creation. Because modernity is based on a certain type of utilitarian and analytic-instrumental reason, creating a rationalistic culture of means with no regard for the ends, suspicion is cast on all other fundamental forms of reason: the reason of the senses, the reason of the heart, our emotional and spiritual intelligence. This latter, of course, is the very seat of ethical perception and spiritual experience, dimensions without which life loses its meaning and luster. These days we need urgently to supplement scientific reason with reason of the heart and of the senses.

Far from having a final resolution in hand, we can at least discern in which direction to go. If we are correct, the way forward may consist of twists and turns, ups and downs, even a few shortcuts, but it will bring us closer to a world where human beings may live in a more human fashion, taking care of one another with compassion and love for the Earth, *Pacha Mama*, our Great Mother.

In this paradigm, one's primary concern would be directed above all toward life, humanity, and the living Earth rather than toward unlimited progress and accumulation of goods. Our economy would serve higher realities. In other words, a bio-civilization would emerge that prefers life over lucre, the collective well-being over individual profits, cooperation over competition. In this way, human beings would become aware that their origin and fate are the same as the Earth's. Our planet would be the Earth of Good Hope, to use the felicitous expression coined by Polish-French eco-economist Ignacy Sachs. In this way we would effect a transition from an industrial civilization that seeks riches by sacrificing nature to a sustainable civilization, where nature and all peoples coexist in osmosis.

I cherish the conviction, shared by other analysts, that the current systemic crisis will leave us, as both legacy and challenge, the need to rethink our relationship with the Earth and our means of production and consumption, so that we might reinvent a form of worldwide governance and a way of coexistence that offers a unique and singular Home to all people. However, it is necessary to reconsider certain key concepts that, like a needle on a compass, will indicate our way to the new, true north. Our current crisis is in great part a consequence of false premises.

Six Concepts That Need a Broader Vision

The first concept that needs revision is development. In practice, it is identified with material growth, measured as gross domestic product. Its dynamic consists of growing as large as possible to infinity, which has led to a pitiless exploitation of the natural world and an increase in national and international inequality. We must abandon such a quantitative understanding and adopt instead a qualitative understanding. The latter defines development, as Amartya Sen put it so well, as "a process of expanding real freedoms," that is to say, an enlargement of opportunities to shape one's own life and to give it a compelling meaning. Growth is inescapable because it is in the very nature of human beings, but growth is only healthy when it is part of a the interdependent networks of life that guarantee biodiversity. Rather than further growth-development, one needs to think of a redistribution of that which has already been acquired or produced.

The second concept in need of revision and implementation is that of sustainability, which in our current system is impossible. In its place we must put the rights of Earth and of nature, as approved by the United Nations. If these are respected, sustainability can be assured as the fruit of an adaptation to a logic of life.

The third concept is that of the environment. It must not be understood in a narrow and local way, nor as merely a container for human life; rather, it must be conceived as the totality of the environment in which all humans live and interrelate—"the community of life," as expressed in the UN Earth Charter. All human beings possess the same basic genetic code, and thus we are all related to one another—a true living community—which implies respect for all human beings as valuable in themselves, beyond any use or function they might serve for others.

The fourth is that of the Earth. It is necessary to go beyond the reductive, modernistic view that sees the earth as an unthinking, material object. As all the journals of ecology report and as contemporary science has shown, the Earth is not simply a place where life exists but it is itself a living being, a super-organism—Gaia—wherein physical and chemical processes along with terrestrial and cosmic energies combine to produce and reproduce life. On April 22, 2010, the United Nations approved the designation "Mother Earth." One does not sell or buy one's mother; one respects and loves her. Thus, the same principle applies to our Mother Earth.

The fifth concept is that of the human being, which in the modern era has been thought of as separate—above and beyond nature. In

Cartesian thought, the definition given was "master and conqueror of the world." Nowadays, human beings are seen more and more as that part of the natural world that feels, thinks, loves, and worships, and so we assume responsibility for the fate of Mother Earth and her children, feeling ourselves together to be companions and caretakers of this small, beautiful, and endangered planet.

The sixth concept is spirituality. Though sometimes delegated to religion, it represents rather the most profound dimension of universal human experience. Spirituality arises from an awareness of one's part in the Whole and from the intuition that every being and the whole universe itself are sustained and infused by a powerful and loving force, the Abyss of all energy, the source of all being. One can sense the mysterious thread that connects and reconnects all things into cosmos and out of chaos. Spirituality inspires awe in us at the wonder of the universe and fills us with self-respect so that we might admire, enjoy, and celebrate all that is.

So much of how we think must be changed until these new habits of thought are a given among us all. But that is what must be—and can be—done.

The Universal Experience of the Sacred

I would like to spend some time exploring a theme more deeply that, as a theologian, is quite dear to my heart. To inaugurate a new covenant with the Earth, one indispensible task is to rescue the sacred. Without the sacred, any affirmation of the *dignitas Terrae* remains useless rhetoric. The sacred constitutes a fundamental experience, one that is the basis for all religion and human culture.

These last few decades have been characterized by systematic interference in the rhythms of nature, to the point that we have become deaf to the musicality of being and blind to the magnificence of the starry sky. We have thereby lost the experience of the sacrality of the universe, and in its place a profanity has insinuated itself that reduces the universe to an inert, mechanical, and mathematic reality and has turned the Earth into a mere department store of resources reserved for our human needs. The holy Word has been removed from every thing, such now mere human words are now all we hear.

If we cannot rescue the sacred, it will be difficult to respect the Earth and the intrinsic value of other human beings. Ecology then becomes a mere technique, an incubator for human voracity, without any further possible use, and this so-called new covenant then would merely be a cease-fire that would perhaps allow the Earth to recover before enduring more assaults, since a model of relationship built upon aggression will not have changed, nor will have our own basic attitudes.

So, before everything else, we must reawaken our capacity to be enchanted by the universe. Here we recall the words of American astronaut Edgar D. Mitchell in 1971 as he was traveling on Apollo 14 toward the moon: "From here, thousands of miles away, the Earth shows the incredible beauty of a magnificent blue and white pearl, floating in a vast, dark sky. It looks like it could fit into the palm of my hand. On it there is everything that is sacred and loved by us."

What is the sacred? It is not a thing. It is a quality of things that overtakes us completely, that fascinates us, that speaks to us about the depth of our being, that evokes in us an immediate experience of respect, awe, and worship.

Rudolf Otto, in his book *The Idea of the Holy*, one of the classics in the study of this subject, describes the experience using two key terms: *tremendum* and *fascinosum*. The *tremendum* is that which makes us tremble before its greatness, because its presence is beyond the human capacity to endure. We flee from it because of

44

its overwhelming intensity. At the same time it is *fascinosum*: it fascinates us, it is an irresistible calamity that draws us to it because of its absolute relevance to our very being. The sacred is like the sun: we are attracted to and delight in its light (*fascinosum*), and yet we must avert our gaze lest we be blinded by its burning light (*tremendum*).

It is this experience of ambivalence that the first human beings experienced and that we, too, can still have in our relationship with the cosmos, with the Earth, with life, with charismatic persons, in the attraction of love between man and woman. The first human beings felt this reality as an invincible force, the *mana* of Polynesian peoples or the *axé* of Afro-Brazilian religions, that all things potentially carry and are revealed as epiphany and diaphany.

Beneath this—as modern cosmologists explain—a source energy is at work, the generative abyss of things, the *Spiritus creator*. The sacred erupts within us when we take in a contemporary vision of the universe in evolution and cosmogenesis. The view of the world provided by Google Maps is not enough. We need to be moved, to experience wonder, to feel ourselves a part of this cosmos, of this Earth, a part of nature, as self-conscious beings with an awareness of our ancestors and our deepest reality. These sorts of emotional experiences are what change our lives.

How can we not feel ecstasy before the immensity of energy emitted from the singularity of the big bang and the formation of the Higgs boson that infused mass into all the original particles of the universe, before clouds of gas, before the formation of the stars, and gave birth to galaxies, stars, planets, and finally our own existence? This is the *fascinosum*.

And what can be even more awe-inspiring and mysterious than the massive destruction of primal material by antimatter that left perhaps merely a millionth part of what originally was, from which emerged our own universe and us ourselves? This is the *tremendum* that accompanies the *fascinosum*, among so many other experiences we might describe.

These facts present us with a truth best understood using a theory of complexity that holds all opposition as complementary and leads us to accept that we ourselves are small parts of a greater whole. Then, we place ourselves into that wholeness and make ourselves at home there, hearing both the harmony and the discordance; we understand that the bass drum and the violin live together; we use our creativity to act in accordance with nature and not against it, to its detriment.

A sense of the sacred brings us back from our exile and relieves us of our alienation. It reacquaints us with the Home that we have left. Only a personal relationship with the Earth can leads us to love her. And when we love, we do not exploit or abuse; we respect and venerate. A new era could begin, not a cease-fire but rather an era of perpetual peace (Kant) and an authentic reconnection with all that is.

We Need a Global Discourse on Ethics

If we take no action, we are in for some very dark times ahead. It is not possible to do nothing. If the wheel cannot be stopped, we must begin, at the very least, to slow it down. We can and we must accept the changes to be made and act to minimize the damaging effects of what we have already done. From this point forward, we must live the four Rs in a radical way: reduce, reuse, recycle, and reforest.

To overcome this crisis, we need a set of ethics that will help orient and guide our behavior. In such a dramatic set of circumstances, how might we establish an ethical discourse that is valid for all people?

Up until now, ethics and morals have arisen from regional cultures, but now, in the planetary phase of our human species, we need to recast ethics using something that is common to all peoples and that all people can grasp and implement. If we examine the past, we can identify two sources of ethics that have guided and still do guide society: religion and reason.

Religion continues to hold a place of privilege among the majority of human societies and is born from the encounter of Supreme Value with the Highest Good. From this is born values of worship, respect, love, solidarity, compassion, and forgiveness. Many consider religion, more than economics or politics, to be the central force that leads people to act, even to the point of sacrificing their own lives (Samuel Huntington). Others have gone so far as to suggest that religion might be the most realistic and effective basis upon which to build a "global ethic for world politics and economies"

TOWARD AN ECO-SPIRITUALITY

(Hans Küng). For this reason, dialogue must take place between the religions of the world, and in this dialogue, commonalities, not differences, must be stressed. This is how peace between religions will be brought forth, a peace that is not an end in itself but that must serve to inspire peace among all peoples.

When critical reason made its appearance in cultures around the world in the sixth century BC, the so-called Axial Age (Karl Jaspers), what emerged were universal ethical codes based fundamentally on a concept of justice but that also affirmed other common values such as freedom, truth, love, and respect for others. This rational foundation for ethics and morals—autonomous ethics—represented one of the more admirable aspects of Western thought put forward in the classical era by Socrates, Plato, and Aristotle; subsequently by Immanuel Kant; and now in our contemporary era by such as Jürgen Habermas, Enrique Dussel, and in Brazil, Henrique de Lima Vaz and Manfredo Oliveira. Nevertheless, the level of influence enjoyed by rational ethics has been modest and confined to certain circles and so has had very little impact on the daily lives of most people.

These two paradigms, the religious and the rational, have not been invalidated by the current crisis, but they each need to be supplemented if they are to be up to the challenge that today's profoundly changed reality presents us. Such an updating requires that we ground ourselves where values are formed, since values are the basis of ethics. If there is to be any consensus at all, ethics must arise from a common basis of all human experience. This basic human experience is not reason, as Western thought has claimed.

Reason—which Western philosophy itself has recognized—is neither the first nor the last moment of our existence, and thus cannot explain everything nor encompass everything. Rather, it provides an opening to what is below, something more elemental and ancestral: affectivity, deep feeling that leaps upward toward the spiritual when we feel a part of the whole, rapt in contemplation and spirituality. For this reason, our basic experience is not "I think, therefore I am," but rather "I feel, therefore I am." Reason (*logos*) is not the root but rather passion (*pathos*), which is expressed through sensibility and affect, and it is from here that a sensible, feeling reason can be recovered (Michel Maffesoli, Adela Cortina). Through this type of reason we can hold the precious character of all that is; it fuels our capacity to desire. A life of value is nurtured from the heart and not from the head, and in that value, we move and we live. In the end, love is the ultimate value, the strongest force in the universe, and the very name of God. This is an ethic that supports our effort to act in concrete ways in response to global warming.

But let's be realistic: a destructive demon lurks within our passion. Passion is a fantastic torrent of energy that, like the water of a great river, needs its banks to regulate and direct its flow, lest it flood and destroy. Here is where the unique function of reason comes into place. Reason is what allows us to see clearly—to order, discipline, and define the direction of passion.

Hence, the dramatic dialogue between passion and reason. If reason suppresses passion, rigidity and a tyranny of order are triumphant. If passion seeks to act without reason, it results in the madness of impulsivity and the mere exploitation of things. But if held in check, passion can use reason to regulate its development and direction, and from this may arise an ethical consciousness that enables us to assume responsibility for ecological chaos and global warming. This is the road we must travel. New times, new ethics.

A New Sense of Meaning

It has been said, rightly, that human beings are driven by two types of hunger: for bread and for spirit. The hunger for bread can be satisfied. The hunger for spirit, however, cannot ever be satisfied, driven, as it is, by impalpable and immaterial values, such as communion, solidarity, love, compassion, an openness toward all that is holy and worthy, and dialogue and prayer directed toward the Creator.

These values, with which all human beings are intimately imbued, know no limits to their growth. An infinite longing is hidden within us, and only an infinite reality can give us peace. If we occupy ourselves with amassing riches and exploiting the material world, we will end up feeling a great void and a great disappointment, as the researchers from the University of Lausanne found out. In the end, we want something greater, something more humanizing.

In this context, therefore, we consider the issue of the meaning of life. Finding one's way toward a coherent meaning for one's life is a basic human need. Emptiness and absurdity produce a kind of anguish, feelings of alienation and loneliness. These days, our industrialized consumer society, built on rational functionality, has placed individual interests at the center, thus fragmenting reality, dissolving any kind of social contract, showing contempt for holy things and ridiculing traditional notions, the so-called great narratives, which get dismissed as essentialist metaphysics from societies of another time. Nowadays, anything goes, and "all is permitted" is the watchword in various types of rationality and various readings of reality, a relativity that asserts, definitively, that nothing has value.

What we call "postmodernism," in my opinion, represents the last and most decadent stage of the bourgeoisie. Dissatisfied with merely destroying the present, it seeks to destroy the future as well. Distinguished by its complete indifference to any transformation of society and by its explicit disinterest in any improvement of humanity, this attitude explicitly denies any solidarity with the tragic fate of millions who struggle to make a decent life for themselves, to live in homes better than the stables and pens of their animals, to have access to cultural resources that could enrich their experience of living. No culture can survive without a common understanding that confers dignity, cohesion, courage, and a collectively shared journey among a people. Postmodernism denies, irrationally, this basic fact.

By contrast, everywhere in the world we see people attempting to make meaning of their lives and of their suffering, looking for a guiding light that might help orient them toward a future worthy of hope. We might live without faith, but we cannot live without hope. Without hope we are only a step or two away from violence, from indifference to death, and in the end, from suicide. With the modern era, those structures that historically provided an ongoing sense of meaning have been eroding. Nowadays, in this planetary phase of human history, no one, not even the Pope or the Dalai Lama, is allowed to say with certainty what is good or bad.

In the course of the last centuries, philosophy and spiritual practices have given answers to what it means to be human, but these days these sources of meaning have largely become rote and have lost their creative juice. They continue to elaborate ever more sophisticated discourse upon that which is already known, rethinking and restating, but not daring to formulate new visions—inspiring dreams and utopian aspirations that might mobilize people into action. We are living in a "malaise of civilization" like that of the latter period of the Roman Empire as described by St. Augustine in *The City of God*. Our "gods" no longer command belief, and the new "gods" on the horizon are not powerful enough yet to be recognized, respected, and placed on our altars. These crises can only be overcome by having a new experience of essential Being through a living spirituality. We see some places in which "new gods" are being announced and a new perception of Being is starting to appear.

For all the numerous critical analyses of globalization on the economic and political level, fundamentally it is an anthropological phenomenon: humanity is discovering that it is a species that lives in a single Home together, sharing a common fate. Such a phenomenon requires global governance to manage collective problems. This is something new.

The World Social Forums, begun in 2000 in Porto Alegre, Brazil, represent a sudden eruption of meaning. For the first time in human history, the poor of our planet, acting in counterpoint to the meeting of the wealthy in the Swiss city of Davos, came together by the thousands to join their forces and share their organizational capabilities in a meeting in Porto Alegre and then, afterward, in other cities throughout the world. At the World Social Forums, the poor describe their experiences of resistance and liberation, they share what they know about developing microalternatives to the dominant system, and they nurture a common dream that cries out, "Another world is possible, another world is necessary." This also is something new.

In the various World Social Forums held on the regional and international levels, we see the seeds of a new paradigm for humanity, capable of organizing production, consumption, stewardship of nature, and inclusivity of all people in a different way, by way of a collective project that would guarantee the future of life and hope for all. This is its importance: from the depths of human neglect has arisen a small wisp of smoke from the interior flame that burns beneath the garbage heap upon which the great majority of humanity has been thrown. This flame is inextinguishable and will grow into a glowing ember, shedding its light on a new sense of meaning for humanity.

Daring to Dream of a Planetary Civilization

I am convinced that our present chaos is creating and generating new possibilities. It is the herald of a new age, an improvement in the history of humanity on the planetary level. Back in 1933, though, the great paleontologist and French thinker Teilhard de Chardin, in China—with his specialized interest in the dynamics of evolution and keen observations on the process of globalization already begun in the areas of commerce, communication, and population—announced the coming of what he termed the "noosphere" (*noûs* in Greek represents the union of heart and mind). He had already observed what we know about globalization: that it is an extension of something quite ancient, representing the progressive elaboration of the complexity of reality that leads to a simultaneous process of interiorization and a growth in the level of reflective consciousness. It had already taken a number of forms: the age of the lithosphere, followed by that of the hydrosphere, the biosphere, and the anthrosphere. Today we are witnessing the advent of a new stage: that of the noosphere.

After humans, humanity. This is the current phase we are in, in which we begun to become aware of being one single human species, a great community made up of a rich variety of peoples who live together in this shared Home that is the Earth. This reality is born of universal forces as much as from human efforts in the course of our evolution forward as a species. To bring this reality into being fully, the Earth must be nourished. Our spirits and our hearts must be united in a common passion and a limitless love for humanity and for the Earth. For this reason, we must revivify our taste for the joy of living, for humanity as a whole, and for our Earth.

As the fruit of ancient stars, we were born to shine, not to suffer: this is why we must shine. This is the purpose of our evolution and the plan of our Creator.

In contrast, the current sense of abandonment that afflicts a large part of humanity comes from our incapacity to dream and envision an ideal world for ourselves—not merely a utopia, but an ideal world capable of being turned into a real and actual *topos*, a place however imperfect that exists within the conditions of our real history. The alternative is that the shared future of our life and civilization is in great danger, so we must not be late in finding the road forward that will save us. This road runs through caretaking, sustainability, and collective responsibility, as well as a spiritual sense of life.

I quote the evocative words of noted Irish writer Oscar Wilde, who, concerning utopia, said, "A map of the world that does not include Utopia is not worth even glancing at, for it leaves out the one country at which Humanity is always landing. And when Humanity lands there, it looks out, and, seeing a better country, sets sail. Progress is the realization of Utopias."

It is part of utopian thought to create scenarios of hope. One such utopian is Robert Muller, who for forty years worked at the United Nations and has been called a "citizen of the world" and the "father of global education." He was a man of dreams, one of which was realized when he created the University of Peace, of which he was the first chancellor. The University of Peace was created by the United Nations in Costa Rica, the only nation in the world without an army. His vision was of a new Genesis: the emergence of a genuinely planetary civilization in which the human species felt itself at one with all others, endowed with the mission to ensure the sustainability of the Earth and to be the caretaker of all living beings that dwelt on its face. Here is an excerpt from Muller's *New Genesis: Shaping a Global Spirituality* (New York: Image Books, 1984).

And God saw that all the nations of the earth, black and white, poor and rich, from North and

South, from East and West and of all creeds were sending their emissaries to a tall glass house on the shores of the River of the Rising Sun, on the island of Manhattan, to study together, to think together and to care together for the world and all its people. And God said: That is good. And it was the first day of the New Age of the earth.

And God saw that soldiers of peace were separating the combatants of quarreling nations, that differences were being resolved by negotiation and reason instead of arms, and that the leaders of nations were seeing each other, talking to each other, and joining their hearts, minds, souls, and strength for the benefit of all humanity. And God said: That is good. And it was the second day of the Planet of Peace.

And God saw that humans were loving the entire creation, the stars and the sun, the day and the night, the air and the oceans, the earth and the waters, the fishes and the fowl, the flowers and the herbs, and all their human brethren and sisters. And God said: That is good. And it was the third day of the Planet of Happiness.

And God saw that humans were suppressing hunger, disease, ignorance, and suffering all over the globe, providing each human person with a decent, conscious, and happy life, and reducing the greed, the power, and the wealth of the few. And He said: That is good. And it was the fourth day of the Planet of Justice.

And God saw that humans were living in harmony with their planet and in peace with one another, wisely managing their resources, avoiding waste, curbing excesses, replacing hatred with love, greed with contentment, arrogance with humility, division with cooperation, and mistrust with understanding. And He said: That is good. And it was the fifth day of the Golden Planet.

And God saw that men were destroying their arms, bombs, missiles, warships, and warplanes, dismantling their bases and disbanding their armies, keeping only policemen of peace to protect the good from the bad and the normal from the mad. And God said: That is good. And it was the sixth day of the Planet of Reason.

And God saw humans restore God and the human person as the alpha and omega, reducing institutions, beliefs, politics, government, and all man-made entities to mere servants of God and the people. And he saw them adopt as their supreme law: 'You shall love the Lord your God with all your heart, all your soul, all your mind, and all your strength. You shall love your neighbor as yourself. There is no greater commandment than these." (Mark 12:30).

And God said: That is good. And it was the seventh day of the Planet of God (pp. 190–91).

If over the door to Hell in Dante's Inferno was written "Abandon all hope, ye who enter here," above the door to the new civilization of the global Age of the Earth shall be written in every language on the face of the earth, "Do not ever abandon hope, you who enter."

The future passes by way of this utopia. And its dawning has already been announced.

Guide for Sharing, Prayer, and Practice

Creation

In prayer:

Boff encourages us to "be taken with wonder" at the beauty of creation. Find something of natural beauty in your environment and take ten minutes to meditate upon it as your prayer today.

For practice:

List on a piece of paper the things in your everyday life that fill you with wonder: objects of the natural world, ways in which the goodness of people has been manifested around you or toward you, how God has come to your assistance in the past or the presence.

In prayer:

Boff urges us to listen to the prophetic call around the thoughtless consumption of our natural resources. In prayer today, reflect upon ways in your life in which you have seen or been party to thoughtless consumption. Hold these instances up to God for forgiveness and healing.

For practice:

As an outgrowth of the prayer practice described above, accomplish three actions today that somehow limit or conserve your use of natural resources.

Relationships

In prayer:

Boff focuses upon the way in which the richest resource of God's creation is not the mere material abundance of the world but what he calls "human capital," the wealth we experience in culture and in relationship to others. Call to mind in prayer today specific people who have enriched your life and give thanks for what they have given to you.

For practice:

An active and thoughtful spirituality nowadays, Boff argues, considers an expansion of freedoms for all people—to receive an education, to earn a decent living, to have adequate access to water and food, to make choices that lead to a fulfillment of oneself. Today's practice is to make a donation—no matter how small—to a worthwhile organization that is working on behalf of these freedoms worldwide.

In prayer:

Boff reminds us of a time in human history when the earth was not experienced as an object but rather as our own personal mother. In prayer today, use this image of Mother Earth in your imagination. How have you felt nurtured by the earth? Are there special ways or places you experience her maternal love and care?

For practice:

As an outgrowth of the above prayer practice, create a small ritual in which you honor God's creation as a Mother. It doesn't need to be extensive or elaborate, but take a moment in some place where you feel the loving, maternal quality of the world and physically do something which gives thanks and reverence

Inspiration and Hope

In prayer:

Boff talks of two aspects of the sacred. The first is the *tremendum*, that which inspires awe. In prayer today, review your own salvation history, the ways in which you have encountered God's awesome power and creativity. Take your prayer time to feel that awe and mystery again within your soul.

For practice:

The second aspect of the sacred is the *fascinosum*, that which enthralls us. Take time today to find a piece of music that you find thrilling and let yourself be lost in its beauty.

In prayer:

Boff ends his book with a beautiful account of a new Genesis from Robert Muller. Let your prayer today be a slow reading of this passage, out loud, paying close attention to which words, phrases and expressions move you. Bring to mind pictures in your imagination that puzzle and challenge you.

For practice:

"Do not ever abandon hope, you who enter" is the motto by which Boff suggests we as a planet and as the people of God move forward. Take a piece of paper and write down as many things as you can that you hope for—personally, socially, and spiritually.

CHURCH AT THE CROSSROAD
A SERIES OF GLOBAL MARKING POSTS

Óscar Andrés Rodríguez Maradiaga
The Challenge of Inequality

Cardinal Rodriguez Maradiaga offers a clear analysis of the expansion of economic inequality and its root causes, followed by a review of suggested solutions, and a hopeful outlook based on new model of economic and human growth.

ISBN 978-0-8245-2081-6
pb / 100 pages

Support your local bookstore or order directly from the publisher at
www.CrossroadPublishing.com.

To request a catalog or inquire about quantity orders,
please e-mail sales@CrossroadPublishing.com.

The Crossroad Publishing Company

CHURCH AT THE CROSSROAD
A SERIES OF GLOBAL MARKING POSTS

Philip Jenkins
The New Map of the Global Church

By 2025, 75 percent of Catholics in the world will be non-European; the new global church will have its center of gravity in Latin America, Asia, and Africa. This fascinating brief explores the metamorphosis taking place in the global community of believers.

ISBN 978-0-8245-2078-6
pb / 100 pages

Support your local bookstore or order directly from the publisher at
www.CrossroadPublishing.com.

To request a catalog or inquire about quantity orders,
please e-mail sales@CrossroadPublishing.com.

The Crossroad Publishing Company

About the Author

Leonardo Boff is a former Franciscan monk, a theologian, and a poet known for his strong voice for the promotion of human rights and ecological responsibility. He is the professor emeritus of ethics, philosophy of religion, and ecology at Rio de Janeiro State University. He is the author of more than sixty books in the areas of theology, spirituality, philosophy, anthropology, and mysticism.

About the Translator

Robert H. Hopcke is the author of numerous works in the field of Jungian psychology and Roman Catholic spirituality. He has translated a variety of books in fields as diverse as art history, sexuality and religion, including most recently, with Paul A. Schwartz, *The Little Flowers of St. Francis*, from Shambhala Publications.

About the Publisher

The Crossroad Publishing Company publishes CROSSROAD and HERDER & HERDER books. We offer a 200-year global family tradition of books on spiritual living and religious thought. We promote reading as a time-tested discipline for focus and understanding. We help authors shape, clarify, write and effectively promote their ideas. We select, edit, and distribute books. Our expertise and passion is to provide wholesome spiritual nourishment for heart, mind and soul through the written word.